Robyn Martin's
best recipes for
crockpots &
slow cookers

Robyn Martin's
best recipes for
crockpots &
slow cookers

photographer James Ensing-Trussell

Chanel & Stylus

Thanks to Smith & Caughey's, Queen Street, Auckland,
and Milly's Kitchen, Ponsonby, Auckland,
for providing crockery for the photography.

First published in 2007 by
Stylus Publishing Ltd and Chanel Publishers Ltd
P.O. Box 403, Whangaparaoa
Reprinted 2008 (twice), 2009

Copyright © Chanel & Stylus
Copyright © text: Robyn Martin
Copyright © photography: Topic Photography

Author photograph on back cover: Syd Mannian
Publishers: Barbara Nielsen and Cliff Josephs
Editorial team: Nicola Farquhar, Diane Lowther
Design and layout: Lesley Coomer

Printed in China through Bookbuilders

ISBN 978-0-9582573-9-8

contents

introduction

If I had to give one small kitchen appliance a medal for versatility and being my kitchen god, my crockpot or slow cooker would get gold. It was a frequent saviour when my children were growing up. It meant I could regularly have the main part of the meal ready when we got home late from after-school activities, work or when it was my turn to cook at the ski club. To open the door, tired and hungry, and smell the dinner cooking is a blessing that definitely puts this appliance in domestic god status. Now that my nest has emptied, my crockpot cooking has reached new heights as I have repossessed my life and do some of the things I dreamed of doing when I had more time.

A clever piece of American marketing in the seventies introduced the world to 'Crock-pots'. This was in fact a brand name for a slow cooker. It soon became every marketer's dream — a generic name for all slow cookers. There are now many different brands, sizes and shapes of slow cookers available and more than 80 million in use. In this book, we refer to all these appliances as slow cookers.

For my money, slow cookers are for people who are time poor or have other things they would rather be doing than worrying about what's for dinner later in the day. They are great for a new mum, enabling her to sort the dinner dilemma in the morning when baby is more likely to be settled. Take the slow cooker to your holiday home and set the dinner cooking in the morning so you can have a holiday from fussing over the meal at the end of the day when you'd rather be relaxing than dealing with the drudgery of meal preparation.

Since slow cookers are for busy people, I have tried to do away with as many unnecessary cooking processes as possible without compromising on flavour. These are mainly things like browning meat and sautéing onions and garlic. If you want to do these things, feel free to, but they are not necessary to achieve great-tasting food in any of my recipes. On this score, I can't see the point of using the slow cooker unless the food can be cooked directly in it. I do use oven bags on a couple of occasions, but even this is not necessary. It just helps the cleaning up!

I have spent many hours experimenting with this wonderful appliance, and I hope you will enjoy the results in this book.

All recipes have been tested in a 4-litre Sunbeam 215–230 watt Slow Cooker.
Standard metric measuring cups and spoons have been used.
1 cup — 250ml
1 teaspoon — 5ml
1 tablespoon — 15ml

the basics

*Understanding what your slow cooker can do will help you
get the most from this versatile appliance.*

- Preheating the slow cooker is not something that fits into my list of things to do and does not make a huge impact on slow cooking times. Speed is not the focus of this style of cooking, however, if you remember, it is fine but not essential to preheat the slow cooker for the recipes in this book.

- You will be amazed how much liquid comes from the food during cooking. If adapting recipes for slow cooking, reduce the liquid by half, adding extra hot liquid towards the end of cooking if necessary.

- Slow cooking makes an excellent job of drawing fat from meat and chicken. You can skim this off before serving using paper towels or a fat sucker, or by carefully pouring it off and discarding it.

- Slow cooking is very forgiving. If the food is ready before you are, turn the slow cooker off and leave it sitting with the lid on until you are ready. The food will retain its heat for about half an hour.

- As a rule of thumb, recipes cooked on LOW can be cooked in half the time if cooked on HIGH, or double the time if the cooking is changed from HIGH to LOW.

- If you need to speed up the cooking time for food being cooked on LOW, turning the slow cooker to HIGH will halve the remaining cooking time.

- The slow cooker cooks using moist heat, so anything that cooks well in liquid or steam will probably cook well in this appliance.

- The slow cooker will not roast, as roasting requires dry heat. It will pot roast however. This is when the meat is browned in the piece then cooked by moist heat in the slow cooker.

- Many meat and chicken dishes do well if they are stirred halfway through cooking. Do this as quickly as possible, as lifting the lid lets the heat escape and can increase cooking time. If it is not possible to stir once during cooking, don't fret. It is not essential.

- There are various opinions on cooking beans in the slow cooker. Despite information to the contrary, I have found haricot beans cook well on LOW for 8–10 hours using boiling water to get the cooking started. Decide for yourself, but my small taste panel liked the beans cooked in this way. You may have to experiment with your slow cooker as results will vary, depending on the wattage and the make of slow cooker.

- Hot or boiling liquids will speed up cooking time.

- It is not necessary to brown meats or sauté onions and garlic for flavour. If you have time and you prefer to do this that is fine but I do not think food cooked in the slow cooker needs this process for great flavour. All the recipes in this book taste fantastic without it.

- Safe handling of food should always be paramount for any cook. Do not leave food to cool in the slow cooker. Place it in a container, cool quickly and refrigerate.

- Salt draws moisture from food, so when possible, add it at the end of cooking.

basic risotto

I have always wanted a way to serve a good risotto to guests without having to go through the time-consuming process of making it when I would rather be with them. Here is my solution! Use this as a basic recipe and add any other ingredients you want for a great risotto.

1 onion
2 cloves garlic
3 tablespoons oil
2 cups risotto rice
4 cups boiling chicken stock

Peel onion and chop finely. Crush, peel and finely chop garlic. Heat the oil in a frying pan and sauté onion and garlic for 5 minutes or until onion is clear. Add rice and cook over a medium heat until the rice turns white. Place rice mixture in the slow cooker. Add the boiling stock. Cover and cook on HIGH for 1 hour, stirring once during cooking if possible.

Serves 4—6

basic stock

2 onions
2 whole cloves
3 carrots
3 stalks celery
1 leek
1kg beef shin on the bone or 2—3 chicken backs or other chicken bones with meat on
1 stem parsley
1 sprig thyme
1 bay leaf
cold water

Peel onions. Press a clove into each. Peel carrots and cut into large chunks. Wash celery and trim. Cut into pieces. Split leek down middle. Wash and cut in half crosswise. Place onions, vegetables, meat or chicken and herbs in the slow cooker. Cover with cold water to about 2cm from the lid rim of the slow cooker. Cover and cook on LOW for 10—14 hours.

Cool and remove fat before refrigerating or freezing.

basic bread

Who needs a breadmaker when you have a versatile slow cooker! This bread keeps well.

15g dried yeast
4 teaspoons sugar
2 1/2 cups warm water
1/4 teaspoon salt
2 cups wholemeal flour
about 4 cups flour suitable for bread making

Place yeast in a small bowl with 1/2 teaspoon of the measured sugar. Pour over 1/4 cup of the warm water and leave to soak for 5–10 minutes. Place remaining water in a large bowl. Mix in yeast mixture, remaining sugar, salt and wholemeal flour. Mix to combine with a wooden spoon. Mix in enough flour to make a stiff dough. Turn onto a floured board and knead the dough until smooth and elastic, working in more flour if necessary. The dough is ready when it springs back after you poke your finger into it.

Oil the slow cooker bowl and place dough in. Cover and cook on HIGH for 2 hours. The bread is cooked when it sounds hollow when tapped. Turn onto a cooling rack. Store unused bread in a plastic bag in the fridge.

tip

The temperature of the slow cooker on the LOW setting is too high to prove the dough without starting the cooking process.

soups

There is little to beat the flavours and nourishment a warming soup can give, and what better way to sensational soup-making than using your slow cooker.

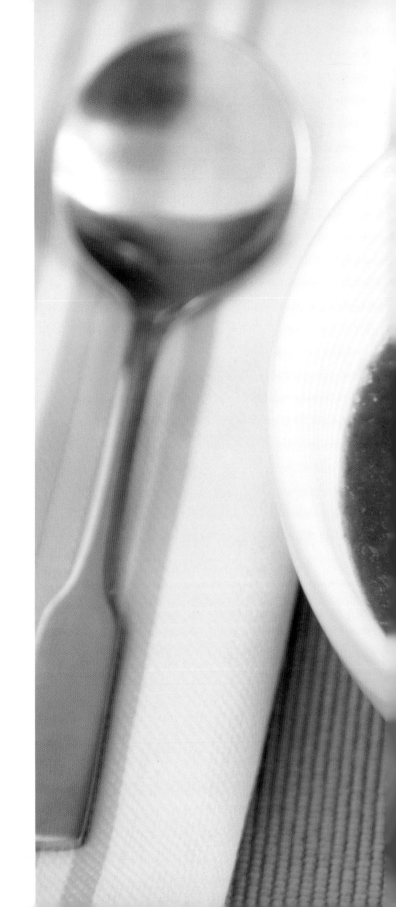

moroccan tomato and capsicum soup

2 onions
2 cloves garlic
2 tablespoons oil
1 teaspoon smoked paprika
1 1/2 teaspoons ground cumin
4 roasted red capsicums
1kg tomatoes
2 1/2 cups chicken stock
basil

Peel onions and chop finely. Crush, peel and chop garlic. Heat the oil in a frying pan and sauté onion and garlic for 5 minutes or until onion is clear. Add smoked paprika and cumin to the pan and remove from heat. Chop roasted capsicums roughly. Remove stem end from tomatoes and chop flesh roughly. Place onion mixture, capsicums, tomatoes and stock in the slow cooker. Cover and cook on LOW for 6–8 hours.

Purée in a blender or food processor. Serve hot, garnished with basil.

Serves 4

farmhouse potato and mushroom soup

Brown mushrooms have better flavour and colour and hold their shape when slow cooked.

2 large onions
2 cloves garlic
4 rashers bacon
8 large, flat, brown mushrooms
6 medium potatoes
3 cups chicken stock
2 bay leaves
1 teaspoon fresh thyme leaves
3 tablespoons flour
2 cups milk
salt
freshly ground black pepper
2 tablespoons chopped parsley

Peel onions and chop finely. Crush, peel and chop garlic. Derind bacon and cut into chunks. Sauté onion, garlic and bacon in a frying pan for 5 minutes or until onion is clear. Remove from the heat. Wipe mushrooms, trim stalks and slice. Peel potatoes and cut into 2cm cubes. Place onion mixture, mushrooms, potatoes, stock, bay leaves and thyme in the slow cooker. Cover and cook on HIGH for 6 hours.

Mix flour to a smooth paste with a little of the measured milk. Add flour mixture and milk. Cook for a further 2 hours. Season with salt and pepper. Serve hot, garnished with chopped parsley.

Serves 4–6

kumara and roasted garlic soup

There is no garlic breath with this soup!

12 cloves garlic	Crush and peel garlic. Peel onions and cut into $^1/_2$ cm rings. Place garlic,
2 onions	onions, salt and oil in a roasting dish, tossing to coat. Bake at 200°C for
$^1/_2$ teaspoon salt	10–15 minutes or until garlic is soft. Peel kumara and cut into 2cm cubes.
2 tablespoons oil	Place roasted garlic and onions, kumara and stock in the slow cooker. Cover
3 kumara	and cook on HIGH for 6–8 hours.
4 cups vegetable stock	Purée in a blender or food processor. Season with salt and pepper. Serve
salt	hot, garnished with crispy fried crumbed onion rings if you wish.
freshly ground black pepper	

Serves 4

carrot, kumara and ginger soup

This soup is delicious with a quarter cup of sweet sherry added half an hour before the end of cooking.

1 onion	Peel onion and chop finely. Crush, peel and chop garlic. Peel kumara and cut
2 cloves garlic	into 2cm cubes. Scrub carrots, trim and cut into 1cm pieces. Heat the oil in
2 kumara	a frying pan and sauté onion and garlic for 5 minutes or until onion is clear.
5 large carrots	Add ginger and chilli and sauté for 1 minute. Place onion mixture, kumara,
1 tablespoon oil	carrots and stock in the slow cooker. Cover and cook on HIGH for 6–8 hours.
1 tablespoon minced ginger	Before serving, purée soup in a blender or food processor, or mash with a
½ teaspoon minced chilli	potato masher. Stir in coriander and serve hot.
6 cups vegetable stock	
3 tablespoons chopped fresh coriander	Serves 6

minestrone

*Red kidney beans must be soaked or precooked before using in a slow cooker recipe.
These beans contain aflotoxins, which are removed in the pre-soaking. This is why you must discard
the soaking or precooking water. These toxins will make you very sick so don't be tempted to try
shortcuts or think you are wasting valuable nutrients when it comes to red kidney beans.
This is not a problem with other commonly used beans.*

1 cup red kidney beans	Soak kidney beans overnight. Drain and rinse, discarding soaking water.
2 carrots	Alternatively, boil for 15–20 minutes, discarding cooking water.
3 sticks celery	Wash carrots and celery and cut into 1cm cubes. Crush, peel and chop
2 cloves garlic	garlic. Derind and chop bacon. Place soaked beans, carrots, celery, garlic,
3 rashers bacon	bacon, savoury tomatoes, tomato paste, chicken stock and bouquet garni in
2 x 400g cans savoury tomatoes	the slow cooker. Cover and cook on HIGH for 6–8 hours.
$1/4$ cup tomato paste	Add macaroni an hour before serving. Slice cabbage finely and add
6 cups boiling chicken stock	to minestrone half an hour before the end of cooking. Season with salt.
1 bouquet garni	Cook for a further 30 minutes. Serve hot, garnished with Parmesan cheese
1 cup macaroni elbows	shavings.
$1/4$ small cabbage	
salt	Serves 6–8
Parmesan cheese	

tip

**Pasta or noodles become pasty with long, slow cooking. This may not bother you but,
if preferred, cook these foods according to their packet directions and add to the slow
cooker just before serving.**

pumpkin and split pea soup

When cooking split peas, always use cold liquid to start the cooking otherwise the peas will stay hard.

1 onion
2 cloves garlic
500g peeled and deseeded pumpkin
2 tablespoons oil
1 cup yellow split peas
5 cups cold chicken stock
salt
freshly ground black pepper
pinch ground nutmeg
basil pesto

Peel onion and chop finely. Crush, peel and chop garlic. Cut pumpkin into 2cm cubes. Heat the oil in a frying pan and sauté onion and garlic for 5 minutes or until clear. Place onion mixture, pumpkin, split peas and chicken stock in the slow cooker. Cover and cook on HIGH for 6–8 hours.

Mix to break up pumpkin and season with salt, pepper and nutmeg. Serve hot, garnished with basil pesto.

Serves 4

tip

The lower the level of food in the slow cooker, the faster the cooking. Ideally, the slow cooker should be half to two-thirds full.

tuscan ribollita, bean and vegetable soup

Ribollita means 'over-boiled' so this is a perfect soup for long cooking in your slow cooker.

2 red onions
2 carrots
2 sticks celery
1 clove garlic
1 potato
2 courgettes
2 x 400g cans Italian-flavoured tomatoes
3 cups boiling water
1 cup haricot or black-eyed beans
2 slices stale bread
4 handfuls baby spinach leaves
salt
Parmesan cheese

Peel onions and chop finely. Peel carrots and cut into $1/2$ cm cubes. Wash and trim celery and cut into $1/2$ cm cubes. Crush, peel and chop garlic. Peel potato and cut into $1/2$ cm cubes. Trim courgettes and cut into $1/2$ cm cubes. Place prepared vegetables, tomatoes, boiling water and beans in the slow cooker. Mix to combine. Cover and cook on HIGH for 6–8 hours.

Half an hour before the end of cooking, break up bread and add to soup with baby spinach. Cover and cook for 30 minutes. Season with salt. Serve hot, garnished with Parmesan cheese shavings and accompanied by crusty bread if you wish.

Serves 6

tip

Acid foods like tomatoes can harden dried beans and some people have found even long, slow cooking will not soften them completely. I have not found this to be the case, but soaking beans or par-boiling them before cooking with acid foods will help prevent this.

bacon and split pea soup

1 onion
2 cloves garlic
2 tablespoons oil
1 carrot
2 sticks celery
1 bay leaf
1 bacon hock
2 cups green split peas
8 cups cold chicken stock

Peel onion and chop finely. Crush, peel and chop garlic. Heat the oil in a frying pan. Sauté onion and garlic for 5 minutes or until clear. Remove from heat. Peel carrot and cut into small cubes. Trim celery and cut into 1cm slices. Place onion mixture, carrot, celery, bay leaf, bacon hock, split peas and stock in the slow cooker. Cover and cook on HIGH for 8 hours.

   Remove hock and cut bacon from bone. Add bacon to the soup, discarding fat, skin and bone. Serve hot, garnished with fresh herbs if you wish.

Serves 6

old-fashioned vegetable soup

Comfort food for winter enjoyment.

1 onion
1 tablespoon oil
500g piece beef shin on the bone
1.5 litres cold water
1 tablespoon beef stock powder
$^1/_4$ cup yellow split peas
2 tablespoons barley
2 sticks celery
1 parsnip
2 carrots
salt
freshly ground black pepper
2 tablespoons chopped parsley

Peel onion and chop finely. Heat the oil in a frying pan and sauté onion for 5 minutes or until clear. Place onion, shin, cold water, stock powder, split peas and barley in the slow cooker. Trim celery and cut into 1cm slices. Peel and grate parsnip and carrots. Add to slow cooker. Cover and cook on HIGH for 6—8 hours.

Season with salt and pepper. Serve hot, garnished with chopped parsley and toasted croutons if you wish.

Serves 4—6

tip

Browning meats before slow cooking adds flavour and colour to a dish, but this takes time and often makes a mess, removing some of the benefits of slow cooking for a time-pressured cook. You can brown the shin meat for this soup for better colour when cooked if you wish.

chicken

Chicken is the perfect ingredient for slow cooking. It stays succulent and has great flavour when cooked in this way. The temperature of the slow cooker is high enough to kill bacteria, making it a safe way to cook chicken.

orange and mango chicken casserole

6 chicken pieces
32g packet onion soup mix
1 cup mango chutney
225g can pineapple pieces in juice
2 tablespoons orange marmalade
1 teaspoon mixed spice
salt

Remove skin from chicken pieces and discard. Place chicken in the slow cooker. Mix soup mix, chutney, undrained pineapple, marmalade and mixed spice together. Pour over chicken. Cover and cook on LOW for 8 hours, stirring once during cooking if possible. Season with salt.

Serves 4–6

chicken paprika

8 boned chicken pieces
37g packet mushroom soup mix
1 tablespoon paprika
125g mushrooms
410g can tomato purée
$1/4$ cup low fat sour cream
salt
1 tablespoon chopped parsley

Remove skin from chicken and discard. Mix mushroom soup mix and paprika together. Wipe mushrooms, trim stalks and slice. Place chicken, soup mixture, mushrooms and tomato purée in the slow cooker. Cover and cook on LOW for 6–8 hours. Stir halfway through cooking if possible.

Half an hour before the end of cooking, mix in sour cream, or spoon sour cream on top of chicken just before serving. Cook for a further 30 minutes. Season with salt. Serve sprinkled with chopped parsley.

Serve 4–6

mexican chicken

This mixture can be used to fill tacos, make burritos or eaten as is, topped with corn chips and grilled cheese. Make a simple guacamole to serve with this deliciously simple brew by mashing a ripe avocado with some lemon juice and a little Mexican chilli powder or minced chilli and a pinch of salt. I like to throw in a crushed, peeled clove of garlic too, which I remove (if I remember) before serving.

6 skinned and boned chicken thighs
35g packet taco seasoning mix
400g can savoury tomatoes
4 corn or flour tortillas
shredded lettuce
grated carrot
grated cheese
guacamole or sour cream

Cut chicken thighs in quarters. Place in the slow cooker with taco seasoning mix and savoury tomatoes. Cover and cook on LOW for 6—8 hours, stirring halfway through cooking if possible.

To serve, warm the tortillas. Top each tortilla with about $1/2$ cup of the Mexican Chicken. Top this with lettuce, carrot, cheese and guacamole or sour cream.

Serves 3—4

tip

There is no rule that says you have to start from scratch when slow cooking. Use prepared mixes such as pasta sauces or packet flavourings to cut down on preparation time.

sweet and sour chicken

8 chicken drumsticks
1 onion
2 sticks celery
1 carrot
1/2 red capsicum
439g can pineapple pieces in juice
2 teaspoons ground ginger
1 tablespoon honey
2 tablespoons white vinegar
1/2 teaspoon Tabasco sauce
2 tablespoons cornflour
2 tablespoons water

Cut the nobbly joint from the drumsticks. Remove skin from chicken and discard. Peel onion and cut into eighths. Separate the onion into separate layers. Trim and string celery. Cut celery into 1cm pieces on the diagonal. Peel carrot and cut into 1cm slices. Cut capsicum flesh into strips. Place onion, celery, carrot, capsicum, pineapple pieces and juice, ginger, honey, vinegar, Tabasco sauce and chicken in the slow cooker. Cover and cook on LOW for 8 hours.

Half an hour before the end of cooking, mix cornflour and water together and stir into chicken mixture. Cook for a further 30 minutes on HIGH. Serve over rice and garnished with coriander if you wish.

Serves 4—6

turkish date and lemon chicken casserole

1kg chicken pieces
1 onion
2 cloves garlic
1 lemon
2 teaspoons ground cumin
1 teaspoon paprika
1 cup chopped dates
1 teaspoon dark brown sugar
$^1/_4$ cup white wine vinegar
$^1/_2$ cup chicken stock
salt
freshly ground black pepper
fresh mint

Remove skin from chicken and discard. Peel onion and chop finely. Crush, peel and chop garlic. Thinly peel rind from lemon. Place chicken, onion, garlic, lemon rind, cumin, paprika, dates, brown sugar, vinegar and chicken stock in the slow cooker. Cover and cook on LOW for 8 hours, stirring halfway through cooking if possible.

Season with salt and pepper. Remove lemon rind before serving. Serve garnished with mint.

Serves 4–6

cajun chicken wraps

*Even roasted nuts become soft during slow cooking. If preferrred,
add them at the end of cooking for extra crunch.*

1 tablespoon Cajun seasoning
32g packet onion soup mix
$1/2$ cup water
1 carrot
6 skinned and boned chicken thighs
$1/4$ cup roasted peanuts
$1/4$ cup natural unsweetened yoghurt
2 tablespoons chopped fresh coriander
4 flour tortillas

Mix Cajun seasoning, soup mix and water together. Peel carrot and grate. Trim any fat from chicken and discard. Cut chicken into 2cm strips. Place soup mixture, carrot, chicken and peanuts in the slow cooker. Cover and cook on LOW for 6—8 hours.

Half an hour before the end of cooking, mix in the yoghurt and coriander. When ready to serve, warm the tortillas in the microwave or oven. Place chicken mixture down centre of tortilla. Fold bottom of tortilla over chicken and wrap around to enclose filling.

Serves 4

tip

Using a packet of onion soup mix saves time peeling and chopping onions and provides thickening and flavour in a slow cooker recipe.

chicken and apricot tagine

1 onion

2 cloves garlic

8 skinned and boned chicken thighs

2 teaspoons ground ginger

1 teaspoon ground cinnamon

1 teaspoon paprika

1 teaspoon ground coriander

1 cup pitted prunes

1 cup dried apricots

$1/4$ cup honey

$1/2$ cup chicken stock

1 teaspoon grated orange rind

$1/4$ cup toasted almonds

2 tablespoons chopped fresh coriander

Peel onion and chop. Crush, peel and chop garlic. Remove any fat from chicken and discard. Cut each chicken piece into thirds. Place onion, garlic, chicken, ginger, cinnamon, paprika, coriander, prunes, apricots, honey, chicken stock and orange rind in the slow cooker. Cover and cook on LOW for 8 hours, stirring halfway through cooking if possible.

Serve garnished with toasted almonds and coriander.

Serves 6

nyonya chicken curry

Nyonya is pronounced 'nonya'. It is the cuisine that came from the marriages of the Chinese and Malay people providing a unique blend of Asian flavours. Nyonya cooking has lemongrass, galangal, an ingredient that looks and tastes similar to root ginger but with stronger flavours of pine and citrus, coconut milk, chillies and limes as essential ingredients.

6 skinned and boned chicken thighs
1 stalk fresh or preserved lemongrass
3 spring onions
1 tablespoon minced ginger
1 teaspoon minced chilli
1/4 cup lime juice
1 teaspoon sugar
1/4 cup coconut milk
1 tablespoon soy sauce
lime wedges

Remove any fat from chicken and discard. Cut chicken thighs in half. Trim the lemongrass, discarding any woody pieces. Cut thinly lengthwise and chop very finely. Trim spring onions and cut into 1cm pieces on the diagonal. Place chicken, lemongrass, spring onions, ginger, chilli, lime juice, sugar, coconut milk and soy sauce in the slow cooker. Cover and cook on LOW for 8 hours, stirring halfway through cooking if possible.

Serve with lime wedges.

Serves 4–6

tip

There is conflicting information about herbs and spices intensifing or losing flavour with slow cooking. The best judge of this is your taste buds, so always taste food towards the end of slow cooking and add herbs or spices to suit.

french chicken

Serve with French bread to mop up the juices, or thicken if preferred.

1 onion
2 cloves garlic
8 chicken drumsticks
1 cup water
1 bay leaf
1 tablespoon mustard seeds
$1/4$ cup capers
$1/2$ cup halved pitted green olives
2 tablespoons prepared wholegrain mustard
$1/4$ cup lemon juice
salt

Peel onion and chop finely. Crush, peel and chop garlic. Cut the nobbly joint from the drumsticks. Remove skin from chicken and discard. Place onion, garlic, chicken, water, bay leaf, mustard seeds, capers, olives, mustard and lemon juice in the slow cooker. Cover and cook on LOW for 8 hours. Stir halfway through cooking if possible.

Thicken if you wish. Season with salt.

Serves 4–6

tip

For a healthier and more attractive result, always remove chicken skin before slow cooking. Palid chicken skin looks unattractive and slow cooking will leach out the fat from under the skin, resulting in a fatty layer on top of the dish.

thai chicken curry

I prefer to use lite coconut milk when cooking. It doesn't seem to compromise the flavour too much and is a lower-fat option for those of us who watch our waistline.

1 onion
2 cloves garlic
6 skinned and boned chicken thighs
1 kaffir lime leaf
2 tablespoons green curry paste
1 tablespoon minced ginger
1 tablespoon Thai fish sauce
400g can coconut milk
$^1/_4$ cup torn basil leaves

Peel onion and chop. Crush, peel and chop garlic. Remove any fat from chicken and discard. Cut chicken thighs in half. Bend lime leaf in several places to extract greater flavour during cooking. Place onion, garlic, chicken, lime leaf, curry paste, ginger, fish sauce and coconut milk in the slow cooker. Cover and cook on LOW for 6–8 hours. Stir halfway through cooking if possible.

When ready to serve, mix in torn basil leaves.

Serves 4–6

tip

The best flavoured curries are often the ones that are cooked long and slow. This makes the slow cooker ideal for creating fantastic curries.

chicken and cranberry casserole

1 onion
2 cloves garlic
8 skinned and boned chicken thighs
3 rashers bacon
170g packet dried cranberries
1 cup red wine
1 teaspoon chicken stock powder
1 bay leaf
3 tablespoons cornflour
3 tablespoons water
salt
fresh rosemary or lavender sprigs

Peel onion and chop. Crush, peel and chop garlic. Trim any fat from chicken and discard. Cut chicken thighs in half. Derind bacon and chop into pieces. Place onion, garlic, chicken, bacon, cranberries, wine, stock powder and bay leaf in the slow cooker. Cover and cook on LOW for 8 hours. Stir halfway through cooking if possible.

Half an hour before the end of cooking, mix cornflour and water together and mix into the chicken mixture. Cover and cook on HIGH for 30 minutes. Season with salt. Serve garnished with rosemary or lavender sprigs.

Serves 6

tip

When using wine for slow cooking choose one that you would like to drink. Cooking does not improve the flavour of a wine so a bad-tasting wine will only spoil the flavour of the dish.

penang chicken curry

2 onions

3 cloves garlic

1 red capsicum

2 teaspoons sesame oil

1 teaspoon ground cumin

1 tablespoon mild curry powder

1 teaspoon mustard seeds

3 skinned and boned chicken breasts

400g can crushed tomatoes in juice

salt

Peel onions and chop finely. Crush, peel and chop garlic. Halve and deseed the capsicum and chop into cubes. Heat the oil in a frying pan and sauté onions and garlic for 5 minutes or until onions are clear. Add cumin, curry, mustard seeds and capsicum. Cook for 1 minute or until spices smell fragrant. Remove from heat. Cut chicken into 2cm-wide strips. Place chicken, onion mixture and tomatoes in the slow cooker. Cover and cook on LOW for 6–8 hours.

Season with salt. Serve garnished with sliced spring onions if you wish.

Serves 4

tip

Read any slow-cooking reference and it will tell you that lifting the lid during cooking adds 20–30 minutes to the cooking time. Apart from recipes for baking, I don't think this matters too much, so if you feel the need for one look or a stir during slow cooking, do so!

green peppercorn chicken

If preferred, the sour cream can be served on top rather than mixed through.

8 chicken drumsticks
1 tablespoon lemon juice
2 tablespoons drained green peppercorns in brine
1 teaspoon prepared French mustard
$1/2$ cup low fat sour cream
salt
parsley

Remove skin from chicken and discard. Place chicken in the slow cooker. Add the lemon juice, peppercorns and mustard. Cover and cook on LOW for 6–8 hours, stirring halfway though cooking if possible.

Half an hour before the end of cooking, add sour cream to the slow cooker, or spoon sour cream on top of chicken just before serving. Cook for a further 30 minutes. Season with salt. Serve garnished with parsley on mashed potatoes if you wish.

Serves 4–6

chicken chilli and basil

I haven't given a spinach measure in this recipe as you can use as much or as little as you have on hand. You can even use thawed frozen spinach if you wish. Spinach needs little cooking so cooking in a slow cooker at the end of cooking is a great way to add the finishing touch to a delicious slow-cooked meal.

6–8 chicken pieces
1/4 cup balsamic vinegar
1/4 cup sweet chilli sauce
3 tablespoons soy sauce
3 spring onions
spinach
1/2 cup fresh basil leaves

Remove skin from chicken and discard. Place chicken, balsamic vinegar, chilli and soy sauces in the slow cooker. Cover and cook on LOW for 6 hours, stirring halfway through cooking if possible.

Trim spring onions and cut into 1cm slices on the diagonal. Fifteen minutes before serving, add spring onions and spinach. Turn the slow cooker to HIGH and cook for a further 15 minutes. Mix in basil leaves and serve.

Serves 4

tip

Sometimes you need to be organised to get the most from your slow cooker. Preparing a dish and refrigerating it overnight ready to put on to cook in the morning can be a stress saver for the time-pressured cook.

it's in the bag lemon chicken

I prefer the tart, zesty light-skinned lemons to those with a bright yellow skin and flesh.
The flavour of this dish will depend on the quality of the lemons you use.

1 medium whole chicken
1 oven bag
2 lemons
2 tablespoons cornflour
2 tablespoons soy sauce
1 tablespoon finely chopped root ginger
salt
fresh herbs
grated lemon zest

Tie chicken legs together and place chicken in the oven bag. Cut lemons into thin slices and place over and around chicken in the oven bag. Mix cornflour, soy sauce and ginger together and pour over chicken. Secure the bag with a heatproof tie. Place oven-bagged chicken in the slow cooker. Cover and cook on LOW for 6–8 hours. When ready to serve, carefully remove chicken from slow cooker and cut the oven bag open along the top, taking care as the steam escapes. Season juices with salt. Serve chicken garnished with fresh herbs and lemon zest.

Serves 4–6

slow-cooked whole pesto chicken

Use store-bought pesto for this or make your own. I like to make a dairy-free alternative with fresh basil leaves, a garlic clove, prepared mustard, capers and enough oil to give the consistency I want, all ground up in a mini food processor.

I medium chicken
¹/₂ cup basil pesto
12 baby new potatoes
¹/₂ cup sundried tomatoes
torn fresh basil leaves

Tie chicken legs together. Place chicken in the slow cooker. Rub chicken with pesto. Wash potatoes and place around chicken. Slice sundried tomatoes and sprinkle over potatoes. Cover and cook on HIGH for 6—8 hours.

To serve, remove chicken from the slow cooker and drain potatoes and sundried tomatoes from the cooking liquid. Toss basil through potatoes.

Serves 4—6

comfort chicken for a cold night

There are lots of ways you can serve this dish. Make buttered crumbs by tossing soft breadcrumbs and melted butter over a low heat until golden and toasted, and use to sprinkle over the chicken before serving. Take a pastry sheet and cut into shapes, bake in a hot oven until golden and crisp and place on top of the chicken mixture to serve. You can always cook this mixture, chill it and make into a pie the next day as another serving option.

4 skinned and boned chicken thighs
1 onion
2 whole cloves
1 bay leaf
2 sprigs parsley
1 sprig thyme
2 fresh sage leaves
1 large carrot
250g button mushrooms
1 cup milk
25g butter
3 tablespoons flour
2 tablespoons chopped fresh parsley
salt

Trim any fat from chicken and discard. Cut chicken thighs into quarters. Peel onion and press cloves into outside of onion. Tie bay leaf, parsley, thyme and sage together with light string or cotton to make a bouquet garni. Peel carrot, trim ends and cut into 1cm cubes. Wipe mushrooms and trim stalks. Place chicken, onion, bouquet garni, carrot, mushrooms and milk in the slow cooker. Cover and cook on LOW for 6—8 hours.

Half an hour before serving, melt butter in microwave and mix in flour to form a paste. Discard onion and bouquet garni from the slow cooker. Mix flour mixture into chicken with chopped parsley. Turn to HIGH, cover and cook for a further 30 minutes. Season with salt. Serve as is or with a crumb or pastry topping of your choice.

Serves 4

tandoori chicken nibbles

2 tablespoons soy sauce
1 tablespoon minced ginger
1 teaspoon minced chilli
1 tablespoon vinegar
2 teaspoons curry powder
1 teaspoon paprika
1 tablespoon apricot jam
1kg chicken nibbles

Mix soy sauce, ginger, chilli, vinegar, curry powder, paprika and apricot jam together. Rub over chicken nibbles and place in the slow cooker. Cover and cook on LOW for 6–8 hours.

 Serve with naan bread or poppadoms.

Serves 6–8

tip

One of the many advantages of slow cooking is that cheap cuts of meat and poultry can be transformed into delicious, tender morsels with a minimum of fuss and expense. Chicken nibbles and wings are inexpensive and make great eating, providing you don't mind picking bones!

normandy chicken

Canned apple sauce is a handy ingredient to have in your pantry. If preferred, you can easily make it from scratch by puréeing stewed apples. This is often a good use for apples that have become soft and mealy with cold storage during the winter.

8 chicken drumsticks
32g packet onion soup mix
350g can apple sauce
4 teaspoons wholegrain mustard
salt
freshly ground black pepper
2 tablespoons chopped parsley
apple slices

Cut the nobbly joint from the drumsticks. Remove skin from chicken and discard. Mix soup mix, apple sauce and mustard together. Place chicken and apple sauce mixture in the slow cooker. Cover and cook on LOW for 6–8 hours.

Season with salt and pepper. Serve garnished with chopped parsley and apple slices.

Serves 4–6

tip

The liquid that will come from chicken, meat and vegetables during slow cooking varies, so you may have to add a little extra liquid. Always add boiling liquid if adding part way through cooking.

moroccan hotpot
with corn bread topping

2 red onions
6 chicken thighs
2 chorizo sausages
400g can Moroccan-style tomatoes
1/2 cup water

Peel onions and slice thinly. Remove skin from chicken and discard. Cut chicken thighs in half. Cut chorizo into 2cm slices. Place onions, chicken, tomatoes and chorizo in the slow cooker. Cover and cook on LOW for 6–8 hours.

One hour before the end of cooking, spoon Corn Bread Topping onto the chicken mixture, spreading to cover. Turn the slow cooker to HIGH and cook for a further hour.

Serves 6

CORN BREAD TOPPING
1 cup flour
1 cup fine cornmeal
4 teaspoons baking powder
2 teaspoons smoked paprika
3 tablespoons chopped fresh coriander
25g melted butter
1 egg
1/2 teaspoon salt
1 cup milk

CORN BREAD TOPPING
Mix flour, cornmeal, baking powder, paprika and coriander together. Make a well in the centre of the dry ingredients. Mix butter, egg, salt and milk together until combined. Pour into dry ingredients and mix to combine.

tip

Adding a bready topping to a slow-cooked dish is an easy way to make something simple into a fantastic taste experience. Use this cornbread topping as a basic recipe and add other flavours if wished.

mango chicken

There are many prepared red curry pastes available at the supermarket and most have a similar flavour profile. Try various brands to establish your favourite. You may find those of Asian origin more authentic.

8 chicken pieces
280ml can low fat coconut milk
1 teaspoon chicken stock powder
1 tablespoon red curry paste
425g can mango slices
1 teaspoon sesame oil
32g packet onion soup mix
2 tablespoons chopped fresh coriander

Remove skin from chicken and discard. Mix coconut milk, stock powder, curry paste, drained mango slices, sesame oil and onion soup mix together. Place chicken and soup mixture in the slow cooker. Cover and cook on LOW for 8 hours, stirring halfway through cooking if possible.

Serve garnished with chopped coriander.

Serves 4—6

latin chicken

Converted white rice has been soaked and par-cooked in its processing, which helps prevent disintegration when it is cooked for long periods. Uncle Ben's is converted rice.

8 chicken drumsticks
1 onion
2 cloves garlic
2 red capsicums
2 cups converted white rice
1 teaspoon smoked hot paprika
400g can diced tomatoes in juice
1 cup dry white wine
2 cups boiling chicken stock
1 bay leaf
1/2 cup stoned black olives
parsley

Cut the nobbly joint from the drumsticks. Remove skin from chicken and discard. Peel onion and chop. Crush, peel and chop garlic. Cut capsicums in half, remove seeds and chop flesh into 1cm cubes. Place chicken, onion, garlic, capsicums, rice, paprika, tomatoes, wine, stock, bay leaf and olives in the slow cooker. Cover and cook on HIGH for 4–6 hours, stirring halfway through cooking if possible.

Serve garnished with parsley.

Serves 4–6

meat

Slow cooking is perfect for meat cookery, turning less expensive cuts into deliciously tender morsels. It's a great way to cook curries too, allowing the flavours to develop as the curry slowly cooks.

slow beef stir-fry

This has all the flavour of a stir-fry, slow-cooked style.
If asparagus is out of season, use green beans.

500g beef blade steak
$1/2$ cup barbecue sauce
2 teaspoons minced ginger
2 tablespoons soy sauce
1 teaspoon sesame oil
1 bunch asparagus or about 10 spears
roasted walnuts

Trim fat from meat and discard. Cut meat into very thin slices. Place in the slow cooker with barbecue sauce, ginger, soy sauce and sesame oil. Cover and cook on LOW for 6—8 hours, stirring halfway through cooking if possible.

Half an hour before the end of cooking, break tough ends from asparagus. Trim asparagus to neaten and cut into thirds. Add to the slow cooker and cook for a further 30 minutes. Serve garnished with roasted walnuts.

Serves 4

slow-cooked beef curry

3 onions
3 cloves garlic
2 tablespoons oil
1 tablespoon minced ginger
3 tablespoons medium curry powder
1kg beef chuck steak
$1/4$ cup flour
1 teaspoon cracked black pepper
$1/2$ cup soy sauce
1 cup beef stock
140g pot tomato paste
mango chutney
cucumber slices

Peel onions and slice thinly. Crush and peel garlic. Heat the oil in frying pan and sauté onion and garlic for 5 minutes or until lightly brown. Add ginger and curry powder and cook for 1 minute or until spices smell fragrant. Place in the slow cooker.

Cut fat from meat and discard. Cut meat into 2cm-wide pieces, 6—8cm long. Mix flour and pepper together in a plastic bag. Toss the meat strips in this. Place meat in the slow cooker with soy sauce, stock and tomato paste. Mix to combine. Cover and cook on LOW for 8—10 hours, stirring halfway through cooking if possible.

Serve topped with mango chutney and cucumber slices.

Serves 6—8

steak and kidney with thyme dumplings

I have to confess that I am not a fan of kidneys. Their smell cooking reminds me of being stuck behind a sheep truck on a long winding road and the texture is like eating high-density foam! How can I get away with saying such terrible things about a food? For those who love kidneys, nothing I say will have any impact on their enjoyment – I know, I live with an offal lover! Here is a modern take on that old favourite.

2 rashers bacon
¼ cup flour
1 teaspoon cracked black pepper
500g steak and kidney, cut into bite-sized pieces
½ teaspoon beef stock powder
1 cup water

Derind bacon and cut into 1cm pieces. Mix flour and pepper together in a plastic bag. Break up steak and kidney and add to flour. Toss to coat. Place bacon, seasoned meat, stock powder and water in the slow cooker. Stir to combine. Cover and cook on LOW for 8 hours, stirring halfway through cooking if possible.

Half an hour before the end of cooking add Dumplings. Cover and cook on HIGH for a further 30 minutes.

Serves 2–4 depending on how much you like steak and kidney!

DUMPLINGS
1 cup flour
2 teaspoons baking powder
1 teaspoon dried thyme
25g butter
about ½ cup milk

DUMPLINGS

Mix flour, baking powder and thyme together. Melt butter and mix into flour. Add enough milk to make a soft dough. Form mixture into tablespoon balls (a measuring spoon is good for this) and drop into steak and kidney.

comfort beef casserole with garlic bread shards

Using a slow cooker when you entertain is a great way to serve fine food with a minimum of fuss. What is more, the slow cooker is very forgiving so if you don't serve the meal exactly when you planned, the risk of the food overcooking is limited.

1kg beef blade steak
37g packet mushroom soup mix
1/4 cup flour
12 pickling onions
12 baby turnips
12 baby carrots
12 brown button mushrooms
1 red capsicum
1 yellow capsicum
1 cup beef stock
1 tablespoon marjoram

Trim any fat from meat and discard. Cut meat into 2cm cubes. Mix mushroom soup mix, and flour together in a plastic bag. Add meat and toss to coat. Peel onions and leave whole. Wash turnips and carrots and trim. Wipe mushrooms and trim stalks. Cut capsicums in half, remove seeds and core and cut flesh into 1cm strips. Place seasoned meat, onions, stock, marjoram, turnips, carrots, mushrooms and capsicums in the slow cooker. Cover and cook on LOW for 8 hours, stirring halfway through cooking if possible.

Serve with Garlic Bread Shards.

Serves 6

GARLIC BREAD SHARDS
1/2 loaf French bread
1 clove garlic
1/4 cup oil
2 tablespoons chopped parsley

GARLIC BREAD SHARDS
Cut bread into sixths lengthwise then cut in half crosswise. Crush, peel and finely chop garlic. Mix garlic, oil and parsley together. Brush over bread slices, place on an oven tray and bake at 200°C for 5 minutes or until golden and crisp.

mushroom-stuffed topside pot roast

This is great for a summer lunch.

1.5kg piece corner-cut beef topside
1 onion
250g brown mushrooms
2 rashers bacon
1 tablespoon oil
1 teaspoon dried thyme
1/4 teaspoon salt
1/4 teaspoon freshly ground black pepper
1 tablespoon honey
1 tablespoon prepared mustard

Trim any silverskin, fat and gristle from the meat. Cut a pocket through the centre of the meat, parallel with the fat side, to about 3cm from edges. Peel onion and chop finely. Wipe mushrooms, trim stalks and slice finely. Derind bacon and chop finely. Heat the oil in a frying pan and sauté onion for 5 minutes, or until clear. Add mushrooms, thyme, salt, pepper, honey, mustard and bacon, and cook, stirring, until mushrooms wilt. Fill pocket in meat with mushroom mixture. Place in the slow cooker. Cover and cook on LOW for 8 hours.

Serve hot or cold, cut into slices. If serving hot, thicken the cooking juices and serve as a sauce with the meat.

Serves 6–8

tip

Pot roasting cooks by the moist heat formed from the water in the food. The meat is often browned first and this can be done if you wish when using the slow cooker to pot roast whole pieces of tougher cuts of meat.

beef shin braise with roast vegetables

$1/4$ cup flour
6 pieces beef shin
12 shallots
2 cloves garlic
2 carrots
3 sticks celery
6 rashers bacon
3 sprigs thyme
1 bay leaf
1 teaspoon cracked black pepper
1 cup red wine
$1/2$ cup beef stock
a mixture of roast vegetables

Place flour in a plastic bag. Add meat and toss to coat. Peel shallots and leave whole. Crush and peel garlic. Peel carrots and cut into 1cm slices. Trim celery and cut into 1cm slices. Derind bacon, cut rashers in half crosswise and roll each bacon piece tightly.

Place meat, shallots, garlic, carrots, celery, bacon rolls, thyme, bay leaf, pepper, red wine and beef stock in the slow cooker. Cover and cook on LOW for 8 hours, stirring halfway through cooking if possible.

When ready to serve, mix in the roast vegetables and serve meat and vegetables with cooking juices spooned over.

Serves 6

crockpot cassoulet

This is a traditional French dish that can be arduous to make. I have modified the cassoulet concept for an easier preparation. This is the sort of dish that is perfect for cooking in a slow cooker.

1 onion
3 cloves garlic
300g piece boiling bacon
2 sticks celery
400g boned lamb shoulder
400g boned pork shoulder
2 cups white haricot beans
2 cups water
8 breakfast pork sausages
140g pot tomato paste
1 teaspoon dried thyme
1 teaspoon ground allspice
1 teaspoon beef stock powder
400g can diced tomatoes
1 bouquet garni
salt
50g butter
2 cups soft breadcrumbs
1/4 cup chopped parsley

Peel onion and chop. Crush and peel garlic. Chop boiling bacon into 2cm cubes. Trim celery and cut into 1cm slices. Trim fat from lamb and pork and discard. Cut meats into 2cm cubes. Place onion, garlic, boiling bacon, celery, lamb, pork, beans, water, sausages, tomato paste, thyme, allspice, stock powder, tomatoes and bouquet garni in the slow cooker. Cover and cook on HIGH for 8–10 hours, stirring halfway through cooking if possible.

Season with salt. Melt the butter in a frying pan. Add breadcrumbs and cook over a medium heat until the crumbs are lightly golden. Serve cassoulet sprinkled with toasted breadcrumbs and chopped parsley.

Serves 6–8

tip

This is a superb dish to serve to guests. It can be slow cooked then frozen for later use, perhaps for a winter dinner party. Thaw in the fridge and reheat slowly, but not in the slow cooker.

turkish lamb pie

This mixture can be eaten as a casserole if you wish.

1 onion
2 cloves garlic
500g piece lamb forequarter
1/4 cup flour
1 teaspoon cracked black pepper
2 teaspoons ground cumin
1 teaspoon ground allspice
1 teaspoon dried marjoram
1/2 cup beef stock
1/2 cup dried apricots
1/4 cup currants
salt
400g flaky pastry

Peel onion and chop. Crush, peel and finely chop garlic. Trim fat from lamb and discard. Cut meat into 2cm cubes. Place flour, pepper, cumin and allspice in a plastic bag. Add meat and toss to coat. Place in the slow cooker with marjoram, onion, garlic, stock, apricots and currants. Cover and cook on LOW for 8 hours, stirring halfway through cooking if possible.

Season with salt. If making into a pie, remove from the slow cooker bowl and cool quickly. When cold, roll half the pastry out and use to line a 20cm pie plate or rectangular fluted tart tin. Spoon in the cold meat mixture. Roll out remaining pastry to make a lid. Trim the edges and use the trimmings to decorate. Make a couple of holes in the centre of the pie for steam to escape. Brush with Egg Wash and bake at 200°C for 20 minutes or until pastry is golden and cooked.

Serves 6

EGG WASH
1 egg yolk
1 tablespoon water

EGG WASH
Mix egg yolk and water together.

tip

You can use a tougher cut of meat for this, buying what is on special at the time. Anything from gravy beef to lean hogget or mutton will become tender when slow cooked.

lamb rendang

*A rendang is cooked long and slow to produce a deliciously tender, full-flavoured curry.
I learnt to make this at a cooking school in Malaysia. Use beef for this if preferred.*

750g boned lamb forequarter
1 onion
3 cloves garlic
$^1/_4$ cup desiccated coconut
3 tablespoons sliced fresh or preserved lemongrass
1 tablespoon minced chilli
2 tablespoons minced ginger
1 teaspoon ground cumin
1 teaspoon ground turmeric
280ml can coconut milk
1 cinnamon quill
salt
chopped fresh coriander

Trim fat from lamb and discard. Cut lamb into 2cm cubes. Peel onion and chop finely. Crush, peel and chop garlic. Place lamb, onion, garlic, coconut, lemongrass, chilli, ginger, cumin, turmeric, coconut milk and cinnamon in the slow cooker. Cover and cook on LOW for 8–10 hours, stirring halfway through cooking if possible.

Remove cinnamon quill and discard. Season with salt. Serve garnished with chopped coriander.

Serves 4

tip

Treat the crock or bowl part of your slow cooker as you would a china or pottery casserole dish. When you remove it from the slow cooker, always place it on a board or hot plate mat. Sudden changes in temperature may cause it to crack.

family favourite lamb shanks

There is something very comforting about a slow cooked meal of lamb shanks. This is a favourite of my family and it is so simple to make. If your lamb shanks are fatty, you can cook them over a low heat in a frying pan first to draw the fat out. Alternatively, skim the fat off the top of the dish at the end of cooking, using paper towels.

1 carrot
2 stalks celery
2 cloves garlic
1 cup brown lentils
6 lamb shanks
425g can savoury tomatoes
2 teaspoons dried Italian herb mix
2 teaspoons minced chilli
$\frac{1}{2}$ cup red wine
salt
fresh herbs

Peel carrot and cut into 1cm pieces. Trim celery and cut into 1cm slices. Crush, peel and chop garlic. Place carrot, celery, garlic, lentils, lamb shanks, tomatoes, herb mix, chilli and wine in the slow cooker. Stir with a wooden spoon to mix. Cover and cook on LOW for 8–10 hours, stirring halfway through cooking if possible.

Season with salt. Serve garnished with fresh herbs.

Serves 4–6

prune and apple stuffed pork rolls

6 pork schnitzel
1 shallot
$^{1}/_{2}$ cup chopped, stoned prunes
1 cup soft breadcrumbs
1 egg
1 teaspoon dried tarragon
350g can apple sauce
1 tablespoon wholegrain mustard
$^{1}/_{2}$ teaspoon salt
freshly ground black pepper

Trim pork, remove and discard any fat. If schnitzel is large, cut in half. Peel shallot and chop finely. Mix shallot, prunes, breadcrumbs, egg, and tarragon together. Place $^{1}/_{4}$ cup of prune stuffing along the short edge of each piece of schnitzel. Roll up to enclose stuffing. Secure with a toothpick if necessary. Place pork rolls in the slow cooker. Mix apple sauce and mustard together. Pour over pork. Cover and cook on LOW for 6—8 hours.

Season sauce with salt and pepper. Serve garnished with fresh herbs if you wish.

Serves 4—6

spicy pork

*Pork fillets are often the most economical way to buy pork as there is little waste. If you prefer –
and the price is better – use some other cut of pork for this dish. The flavours are superb so it doesn't
matter if the pork is in a piece or in cubes. There may be a little extra moisture from cubed pork.
If this bothers you, thicken the cooking juices if you wish.*

2 pork fillets
4 shallots
1 tablespoon yellow or black mustard seeds
1 tablespoon minced chilli
$^1/_2$ teaspoon ground cumin
1 teaspoon ground turmeric
1 tablespoon brown sugar
$^1/_4$ cup fresh lime juice
1 kaffir lime leaf

Trim meat if necessary. Cut each fillet in half crosswise. Peel shallots and chop finely. Place pork, shallots, mustard seeds, chilli, cumin, turmeric, brown sugar, lime juice and crushed kaffir lime leaf in the slow cooker. Cover and cook on LOW for 8 hours, stirring halfway through cooking if possible.

When ready to serve, remove the pork fillets from the slow cooker and slice thickly. Serve on noodles if you wish, with sauce spooned over and garnished with fresh herbs if you wish.

Serves 4

clove and orange glazed 'ham'

One of my early crockpot successes was cooking boiling bacon in this wonderful appliance. It cooks to perfection and is so easy to just finish off under the grill if you want something that looks special. There is no reason why a good piece of boiling bacon cannot be used as a ham substitute for special occasions, especially when you want to serve it hot and perhaps when there is not a large group to feed. This is certainly worth trying as it is very delicious!

I piece boiling bacon or pickled pork, about 1kg
hot water
about 20 whole cloves
cranberry sauce

Place boiling bacon in the slow cooker and cover with hot water. Cover and cook on LOW for 6–8 hours.

Remove from the slow cooker and drain. Remove skin. Score a diamond pattern on the surface and stud with whole cloves. Spread Glaze over. Place in a roasting dish or grill pan and grill until golden, taking care not to put meat too close to the element or you may burn this sugary mixture. Serve hot or cold with cranberry sauce or a mixture of cranberry sauce and orange marmalade.

Serves 6

GLAZE
1 tablespoon orange marmalade
2 teaspoons orange juice
2 tablespoons dark brown sugar
$1/2$ teaspoon prepared mustard

GLAZE

Mix the orange marmalade, orange juice, sugar and mustard together until combined.

mac's oxtail stew

Oxtail used to be a cheap meat cut but, as with lamb shanks, restaurateurs have made them trendy, pushing the price up as a result. Oxtails are not always easy to buy, so you may have to order one from your butcher if you want to experience the delicious flavours of this stew.

1 oxtail
2 tablespoons flour
1 tablespoon cracked black pepper
39g packet oxtail soup mix
1 clove garlic
1 tablespoon Worcestershire sauce
2 bay leaves
1 cup dark beer
fresh herbs

If the butcher has not already cut the oxtail into segments, use a sharp knife to do this. Mix flour, pepper and oxtail soup together in a plastic bag. Add oxtail and toss to coat. Crush, peel and finely chop garlic. Place oxtail, garlic, Worcestershire sauce, bay leaves and beer in the slow cooker. Cover and cook on LOW for 10–12 hours.

Garnish with fresh herbs and serve with baked or mashed potatoes.

Serves 4–6

ancona trippa

If there is one country that does tripe well it has to be Italy, and while I am aware that there are many people who would never consider eating tripe, I am also aware that those who do are totally passionate about their tripe experiences. I have walked the streets of Florence in searing 40°C plus temperatures with my offal lover, looking for a restaurant that served tripe. He is still talking about it!

1kg tripe
1 onion
2 cloves garlic
1 tablespoon oil
1 large carrot
2 sticks celery
1 lemon
1 teaspoon dried marjoram
1 ham or bacon bone
140g pot tomato paste
1 cup water
salt
Parmesan cheese
toasted crusty bread
olive oil

Wash tripe in cold water. Place in a large saucepan, cover with cold water and bring to the boil. Drain and rinse in cold water. Cut tripe into strips about 4cm long and 1–2cm wide. Peel onion and chop finely. Crush, peel and chop garlic. Heat the oil in a frying pan and sauté onion and garlic for 5 minutes or until clear. Peel carrot and cut into 1cm cubes. Trim celery and cut into 1cm slices. Thinly pare rind from lemon. Place tripe, onion mixture, carrot, celery, lemon rind, marjoram, ham bone, tomato paste and water in the slow cooker. Cover and cook on LOW for 8 hours, stirring halfway through cooking if possible.

Season with salt. Garnish with Parmesan cheese and serve with toasted crusty bread dipped in olive oil.

Serves 4–6

mince & sausages

Where would we be without mince and sausages to add interest to our everyday meals! Change the flavour of these dishes by using different flavoured sausages or varying the type of mince used.

cannelloni in rich tomato sauce

2 cubes frozen spinach, or
1 cup frozen free-flow spinach
500g lean beef mince
1/2 cup soft breadcrumbs
1 teaspoon dried basil
pinch ground nutmeg
1/2 teaspoon prepared minced chilli
12 dried pasta cannelloni tubes
oil spray
2 x 400g cans Italian-flavoured tomatoes
3 tablespoons tomato paste
1/2 cup chopped sundried tomatoes
Parmesan cheese shavings

Thaw spinach and squeeze out any extra moisture if necessary. Mix spinach, mince, breadcrumbs, basil, nutmeg and chilli together until combined. Use this mixture to fill cannelloni tubes. Spray the inside of the slow cooker bowl with oil. Place filled pasta in the slow cooker. Mix tomatoes, tomato paste and sundried tomatoes together. Pour over cannelloni. Cover and cook on LOW for 4–6 hours.

Serve garnished with Parmesan cheese.

Serves 4–6

curried sausages with mango

Slow cooking provides a no-fuss way to make this popular, delicious family meal.

2 sticks celery
8 pork sausages
425g can mangoes
1 tablespoon madras curry powder
1 teaspoon yellow mustard seeds
1 cup chicken stock
32g packet onion soup mix
mango chutney
chopped fresh coriander

Trim celery and cut into 1cm pieces. Place sausages, celery, drained mangoes, curry powder and mustard seeds in the slow cooker. Mix stock and onion soup mix together and pour over sausages. Cover and cook on LOW for 6–8 hours, stirring halfway through cooking if possible.

Serve sausages cut in half diagonally, with steamed rice, accompanied by mango chutney and garnished with chopped coriander.

Serves 4–6

mexican meatloaf

This can be served in slices or wedges as you would a meat loaf.
It does not have to be served in a tortilla.

1 onion
500g beef mince
250g sausagemeat
140g pot tomato paste
1 tablespoon Mexican chilli powder
435g can refried beans
2 eggs
oil spray
tortillas
tomato relish

Peel onion and chop finely. Mix onion, mince, sausagemeat, tomato paste, chilli powder, refried beans and eggs together until well combined. Clean or plastic-gloved hands are good for this mixing. Spray the inside of the slow cooker bowl with oil. Press the meat mixture into the bowl. Cover and cook on LOW for 6–8 hours.

When ready to serve, run a knife around the edge of the loaf and turn onto a board. Serve hot or cold, cut into wedges or slices. Serve in a tortilla with tomato relish and salad vegetables if you wish.

Serves 6

tip

Cheap mince is inexpensive for one reason – it contains more fat! Buying cheap mince is false economy and is not a good habit when making a meat loaf in the slow cooker, especially if you plan to eat it cold. The fat will come out during cooking and solidify around and between the meat in the loaf when it's cold.

vietnamese pork balls

1 clove garlic
1 shallot
500g lean pork mince
1/2 teaspoon sugar
1 tablespoon finely chopped fresh
or preserved lemongrass
1 tablespoon fish sauce
1 teaspoon minced chilli
fresh herbs

Crush, peel and finely chop garlic. Peel and finely chop shallot. Mix garlic, shallot, mince, sugar, lemongrass, fish sauce and chilli together until well combined. Form tablespoons of mixture into balls and place in the slow cooker. Pour Sauce over. Cover and cook on LOW for 6—8 hours.

Serve garnished with fresh herbs on a bed of noodles.

Serves 4

SAUCE
1 clove garlic
1 tablespoon fish sauce
1/2 teaspoon minced chilli
1/4 cup fresh lime juice
1 teaspoon sugar

SAUCE
Crush, peel and finely chop garlic. Mix garlic, fish sauce, chilli, lime juice and sugar together.

savoury mince and eggplant bake

This is inspired by moussaka. It is a great way to use your slow cooker for something a little different from the casserole-style meals it is so good at making.

1 onion
2 cloves garlic
500g minced lamb
700g jar tomato and herb pasta sauce
140g pot tomato paste
1 medium eggplant
2 eggs
250g pot ricotta cheese
$^1/_2$ cup milk
$^1/_2$ teaspoon salt
freshly ground black pepper
$^1/_4$ cup grated Parmesan cheese

Peel onion and chop finely. Crush, peel and chop garlic. Combine onion, garlic, lamb mince, pasta sauce and tomato paste. Wash eggplant and cut into 1cm slices. Place a layer of eggplant over the base of the slow cooker. Cover with a layer of the mince mixture. Repeat the layering, finishing with a layer of eggplant. Beat eggs, ricotta, milk, salt and pepper together. Pour over eggplant. Sprinkle with Parmesan cheese. Cover and cook on LOW for 8—10 hours or until top is set. Do not cook this dish on HIGH.

Serve hot or cold, cut into wedges, with a green salad.

Serves 6—8

pork and chicken liver terrine

Try this for alfresco dining.

4 shallots
3 cloves garlic
250g chicken livers
1 teaspoon dried thyme
1 1/2 teaspoons dried tarragon
1 teaspoon dried rosemary leaves
1/4 cup brandy
1/2 teaspoon salt
1 teaspoon cracked black pepper
250g pork sausagemeat
250g pork mince
1/2 cup shelled pistachios
10 rashers streaky bacon

Peel shallots and chop roughly. Crush and peel garlic. Trim sinews and fat from chicken livers and discard. Place shallots, garlic, chicken livers, thyme, tarragon, rosemary, brandy, salt and pepper in the bowl of a food processor and process until coarsely chopped. Add sausagemeat, mince and pistachios and pulse processor until mixture is just combined.

Line the bowl of the slow cooker with bacon, so the bacon extends to the top edge of the bowl. Carefully spread the pork mixture into the bowl, spreading it to the edge. Fold bacon over the top of the pork mixture. Cover and cook on LOW for 6–8 hours.

Carefully run a knife around the edge of the bowl and turn terrine onto a board. Wrap in foil and refrigerate until ready to serve. Serve sliced with French bread and olives if you wish.

Serves 10 as a starter

tip

If the bowl of your slow cooker becomes stained, try cleaning it by adding 1 cup of white vinegar and filling the bowl with hot water, then heating on HIGH for 2 hours.

barbecue-style sausages

When the weather makes barbecuing a distant memory, these sausages will remind you just how good those summer barbecue flavours can be. Use your favourite flavour of sausages for this recipe.

8 sausages
400g can savoury tomatoes
3 tablespoons tomato paste
2 tablespoons white vinegar
2 tablespoons brown sugar
1 tablespoon prepared mustard
2 tablespoons Worcestershire sauce
$^1/_2$ cup beef stock

Place sausages in the slow cooker. Mix savoury tomatoes, tomato paste, vinegar, brown sugar, mustard, Worcestershire sauce and stock together. Pour over sausages. Cover and cook on LOW for 6–8 hours.

Serve with a green salad.

Serves 4–6

tip

The bowl of the slow cooker is not flameproof so it cannot be used over the direct heat of a gas flame or electric element without breaking.

one-pot meals

A one-pot meal has got to be the answer to a dishwasher's prayer. There is only the slow cooker to wash up after a meal like this.

prune and orange lamb shanks

Don't be confused with plums and prunes – prunes are dried plums.
Orange-flavoured prunes are labelled as orange-flavoured plums.

4 large lamb shanks
3 onions
2 cloves garlic
3 medium kumara
1 sprig rosemary
1 cup orange-flavoured plums
$^1\!/_2$ cup orange marmalade
1 cup red wine
$^1\!/_2$ cup beef stock
2 bunches broccolini
orange slices

Trim any fat from shanks and discard. Peel onions and chop finely. Crush, peel and chop garlic. Peel kumara and cut into 2cm chunks. Place shanks, onions, garlic, kumara, rosemary, plums, marmalade, wine and stock in the slow cooker. Cover and cook on LOW for 8–10 hours.

Half an hour before ready to serve, turn slow cooker to HIGH. Trim broccolini and add to slow cooker. Cook for a further 20–30 minutes or until just cooked. Serve garnished with orange slices.

Serves 4

chicken sausages with apple and couscous

I am amazed how well couscous stands up to slow cooking. Israeli couscous
can be used instead of regular couscous if you wish.

2 leeks
3 apples
1 cup couscous
8–12 chicken sausages
3 tablespoons wholegrain mustard
1 cup cold chicken stock
fresh herbs

Trim leeks, split down the centre and wash well between layers. Cut leeks into 1cm slices. Peel, core, quarter and slice apples. Layer leeks, apples and couscous in the slow cooker. Top with sausages. Mix mustard and chicken stock together and pour over sausages. Cover and cook on LOW for 8 hours.

Serve garnished with fresh herbs and accompanied by mustard pickles if you wish.

Serves 4–6

malaysian beef with vegetables and noodles

Dishes like this are cooked in the food halls of Asia. They are a complete meal, usually eaten with chopsticks and a spoon to enjoy the delicious cooking stock. Other green vegetables can be used, just add them in sufficient time to allow them to cook. Vegetables like bok choy and choy sum are very good in these dishes.

1 onion

2 cloves garlic

1 tablespoon oil

1 tablespoon minced ginger

2 teaspoons minced chilli

350g blade steak

400g can Indian-flavoured tomatoes

2 cups beef stock

2 bundles instant noodles

4 large handfuls baby spinach leaves

Peel onion and chop finely. Crush, peel and chop garlic. Heat the oil in a frying pan and sauté onion and garlic for 5 minutes or until onion is clear. Remove from heat and mix in ginger and chilli. Cut meat into 1cm-wide strips. Place onion mixture, meat, tomatoes and stock in the slow cooker. Cover and cook on LOW for 6–8 hours.

Fifteen minutes before you are ready to serve, turn the slow cooker to HIGH and add the noodles. Cook for a further 15 minutes. Add spinach just before serving. Serve sprinkled with chopped coriander if you wish.

Serves 4

tip

When a slow-cooker recipe calls for a specific cut of meat, feel free to use your discretion, depending on what is readily available or what is the best price. Suitable substitutes for blade steak include chuck, skirt or topside steaks, or even gravy beef.

all-in-the-pot corned beef with vegetables

12 small gourmet potatoes
12 baby carrots
1 onion
1.5kg piece corned beef
hot water
1 tablespoon vinegar
2 tablespoons brown sugar
12 black peppercorns
6 whole cloves
1 bay leaf
$^1/_2$ small cabbage
mustard

Wash potatoes. Trim carrots and wash. Peel onion and cut into quarters. Place vegetables and meat in the slow cooker. Cover with hot water. Add vinegar, brown sugar, peppercorns, cloves and bay leaf. Cover and cook on LOW for 6—8 hours.

Fifteen minutes before the end of cooking, turn the slow cooker to HIGH. Wash cabbage and cut into 6 wedges. Place on top of the liquid in the slow cooker. Cook for a further 10 minutes.

Serve the corned beef sliced, accompanied by the drained vegetables and with mustard.

Serves 4—6

creamy corn and vegetable bake with crispy bacon

*This is a great dish to serve for a lighter-style meal on a Sunday night.
It makes an excellent lunch dish too.*

500g bag frozen whole kernel corn
$^1/_2$ cup flour
3 courgettes
2 tomatoes
1 onion
2 cloves garlic
1 tablespoon oil
1 cup milk
$^1/_2$ teaspoon salt
freshly ground black pepper
1 cup grated tasty cheese
8 rashers middle or streaky bacon
4 toasted, serving-sized pieces focaccia or ciabatta bread

Thaw corn. Toss corn in flour and place in the slow cooker. Trim courgettes and grate coarsely. Remove core from tomatoes and chop flesh roughly. Mix courgettes and tomatoes into corn. Peel onion and chop finely. Crush, peel and finely chop garlic. Heat the oil and sauté onion and garlic for 5 minutes, or until clear. Add to vegetables. Mix milk, salt, pepper and cheese together. Pour over vegetables. Cover and cook on LOW for 4–6 hours.

When ready to serve, grill or microwave bacon until crisp and golden. Serve the corn mixture on toasted focaccia or ciabatta bread, topped with bacon.

Serves 4

tip

Ingredients that have been frozen can be used in slow cooking but they must be thawed first. It is best to thaw frozen foods slowly in the refrigerator.

baked stuffed capsicums with tomato and vegetable sauce

I have to confess that stuffed vegetables have never really featured in my culinary repertoire. They always seemed a bit old fashioned and fiddly to prepare yet I always enjoy eating them when someone else has gone to the trouble to make them. They cook perfectly in the slow cooker so I have sorted my prejudices and these are now a feature in our meals.

8 even-sized large red capsicums
1 onion
2 cloves garlic
2 tablespoons oil
4 cups soft breadcrumbs
1 egg
6 anchovy fillets
1 tablespoon capers
1 tablespoon dried Italian herbs
1 cup grated mozzarella cheese
1/4 cup grated Parmesan cheese
2 courgettes
2 carrots
400g can Italian-flavoured tomatoes

Cut top from capsicums and remove core. Peel onion and chop finely. Crush, peel and chop garlic. Heat the oil in a frying pan and sauté onion and garlic for 5 minutes, or until clear. Mix onion mixture, breadcrumbs, egg, anchovies, capers and herbs together until combined. Use to fill the capsicums. Mix the cheeses together and top the stuffing with this. Trim courgettes and grate. Peel carrots and grate. Mix courgettes and carrots into tomatoes and pour around the capsicums. Cover and cook on LOW for 4 hours.

Serve with crusty bread to mop up the juices if you wish.

Serves 4

venison hotpot

Enjoy this around a cheery fire on a cold winter's night.

500g venison
¹/₄ cup flour
1 teaspoon cracked black pepper
¹/₂ teaspoon ground ginger
1 onion
2 cloves garlic
2 rashers bacon
1 swede
¹/₂ cup red wine
¹/₄ cup red wine vinegar
4 cubes frozen spinach or 2 cups frozen free-flow spinach
¹/₄ cup redcurrant or whole cranberry jelly

Trim any fat from venison and discard. Cut meat into 2cm cubes. Mix flour, pepper and ginger together in a plastic bag. Add meat and toss to coat. Place the meat in the slow cooker.

Peel onion and chop finely. Crush, peel and chop garlic. Derind bacon and chop roughly. Peel swede and cut into 1cm cubes. Add onion, garlic, bacon, wine, vinegar and swede. Cover and cook on LOW for 6–8 hours.

Half an hour before the end of cooking, turn the slow cooker to HIGH. Add frozen spinach, pressing into the hot meat mixture. Cook for a further 30 minutes. Stir well before serving, topped with redcurrant or cranberry jelly.

Serves 4

tip

The slow cooker is ideal for cooking game as it usually requires long, slow cooking. Wild or farmed venison can be used for this dish, or wild pig would make a delicious substitute and cook perfectly in the slow cooker.

vegetarian

These dishes prove that vegetarian food need not be dull and tasteless. They are so tasty that non-vegetarians too will enjoy the pleasures of a meatless meal.

roasted capsicum and eggplant lasagne

This dish produces a reasonable amount of liquid from the vegetables as it cooks. If preferred, the vegetables can be tossed in flour before layering, to thicken the juices slightly.

6 roasted red capsicums
1 medium eggplant
3 courgettes
400g packet fresh lasagne sheets
400g can Italian-flavoured tomatoes
250g pot ricotta or cottage cheese
1 cup grated mozzarella cheese
1/4 cup grated Parmesan cheese

Cut capsicums into strips. Cut eggplant into 1cm slices. Cut courgettes in half lengthwise. Cut lasagne into rounds to fit the slow cooker bowl. Use off-cuts to fit if necessary.

Oil the slow cooker bowl. Place a layer of vegetables on the base of the bowl. Pour a thin layer of tomatoes over this then top with a sheet of lasagne. Repeat the layers, finishing with a layer of tomatoes. Mix the cheeses together and sprinkle over tomatoes. Cover and cook on LOW for 6 hours.

Serve with a green salad.

Serves 4

slow-cooked pumpkin tarte tatin

4 onions
3 red capsicums
2 yellow capsicums
3 cups grated pumpkin
1 egg
1 teaspoon Moroccan spice
tomato relish
Parmesan cheese shavings

Peel onions and slice finely. Cut capsicums in half, remove core and seeds and cut flesh into 0.5cm slices. Arrange over the bottom of the slow cooker. Mix pumpkin, egg and Moroccan spice together and spread over capsicums and onions. Cover and cook on LOW for 6 hours.

Serve with tomato relish and Parmesan cheese.

Serves 4

potato, olive and pesto pie

oil spray
1/4 cup toasted breadcrumbs
6 medium potatoes suitable for mashing
1/2 cup basil pesto
1 cup chopped sundried tomatoes
1 cup pitted black olives
1/4 cup vegetable stock
1 cup grated tasty cheese
fresh basil

Spray the inside of the slow cooker bowl with oil. Sprinkle breadcrumbs over. Peel potatoes and slice very thinly using the slicer on your grater, a sharp knife, or the food processor. Arrange about one-third of the potatoes over the base of the slow cooker. Spread with half of the pesto and sprinkle with half of the sundried tomatoes and black olives. Repeat with remaining ingredients, finishing with a layer of potato. Pour stock over. Sprinkle with grated cheese. Cover and cook on LOW for 6 hours.

Serve with Basil Aïoli and garnish with basil.

Serves 4–6

BASIL AÏOLI
1/2 cup aïoli
3 tablespoons finely chopped fresh basil

BASIL AÏOLI
Mix aïoli and basil together.

chilli beans and vegetables

This recipe was cooked on LOW and produced soft, edible beans. If you are not sure about bean cooking in your slow cooker, cook on HIGH for 4–5 hours. If Indian-flavoured tomatoes are not available, use canned chopped tomatoes and add curry powder or paste to taste.

2 onions
2 cloves garlic
2 tablespoons oil
1 teaspoon minced chilli
1 teaspoon red curry paste
1 kumara
250g brown mushrooms
1 cup haricot or black eyed beans
2 cups boiling water
400g can Indian-flavoured tomatoes
chopped fresh coriander

Peel onions and chop finely. Crush, peel and chop garlic. Heat the oil in a frying pan and sauté onion and garlic for 5 minutes, or until clear. Remove from heat and mix in chilli and curry paste. Peel kumara and cut into 2cm pieces. Wipe mushrooms, trim stalks and slice if large. Place onion mixture, kumara, mushrooms, beans, boiling water and tomatoes in the slow cooker. Cover and cook on LOW for 8–10 hours.

Serve garnished with chopped coriander.

Serves 4

tuna and bulgur stuffed buttercup

Use this recipe as a basic concept, changing the flavour by using different flavoured canned tomatoes or adding fresh herbs and other spices you enjoy.

2 sheets baking paper long enough to go from one side to the other of the slow cooker plus a bit extra

1 buttercup about 20cm in diameter

2 courgettes

158g can tuna in spring water

$1/2$ cup bulgur wheat

2 teaspoons grated lemon rind

2 tablespoons capers

400g can savoury tomatoes

2 teaspoons minced chilli

1 teaspoon salt

freshly ground black pepper

avocado and lime oil (if not available, add $1/2$ teaspoon grated lime rind to avocado or olive oil)

fresh herbs

Fold baking paper lengthwise into eighths. Run the strips from one side of the slow cooker to the other at right-angles to each other. This will be used to easily remove the buttercup from the cooker when it is cooked.

Wash buttercup and dry. Cut top off buttercup, about 4cm down. Scoop out seeds. Trim courgettes and grate coarsely. Mix courgettes, drained tuna, bulgur, lemon rind, capers, tomatoes, chilli, salt and pepper together. Use to fill the buttercup. Replace the top of the buttercup. Place buttercup in the slow cooker. Cover and cook on LOW for 6–8 hours.

Using the baking paper, carefully remove buttercup from the slow cooker and place on a board. Cut into wedges. Serve drizzled with avocado oil and garnished with fresh herbs.

Serves 6

vegetable and chickpea curry

1 onion
2 cloves garlic
2 tablespoons oil
2 potatoes
2 carrots
400g deseeded pumpkin
1 cup chickpeas
400g can low fat coconut milk
1 tablespoon red curry paste
1 cup boiling water
1 bunch spinach (optional)

Peel onion and chop finely. Crush, peel and chop garlic. Heat the oil in a frying pan and sauté onion and garlic for 5 minutes, or until clear. Peel potatoes, carrots and pumpkin and cut into 2cm cubes. Place onion mixture, prepared vegetables and chickpeas in the slow cooker. Mix coconut milk, curry paste and boiling water together and pour over vegetables in the slow cooker. Cover and cook on HIGH for 6–8 hours.

If using the spinach, 10 minutes before the end of cooking, wash spinach and discard stems. Add spinach leaves to the slow cooker and cook for a further 10 minutes. Serve with Cucumber Raita.

Serves 4

CUCUMBER RAITA
1/2 cucumber
1/2 teaspoon salt
1/2 cup natural unsweetened yoghurt
1 tablespoon fresh lime juice
2 teaspoons chopped fresh coriander

CUCUMBER RAITA
Cut cucumber in half and discard seeds. Cut cucumber flesh into very small cubes. Place in a bowl and sprinkle with salt. Leave to stand for 15 minutes. Drain well. Mix into yoghurt with lime juice and coriander.

tip

When cooking vegetables such as carrots, potatoes, kumara, turnips, swede and parsnip, place them on the base and sides of the slow cooker as they tend to take longer to cook.

desserts

No one was more surprised than I was at how well the slow cooker cooks these desserts, making it a truly versatile appliance.

chocolate dessert cake

This is a fantastic 'cake' for entertaining.

500g cooking chocolate
6 eggs
1 cup cream
1 1/2 cups toasted ground almonds
icing sugar
fruit

Melt chocolate in the microwave to packet directions or stand in a bowl over hot water until melted. Break eggs into a bowl and stand over hot water for 5 minutes. Beat eggs until light and thick. Whip cream until soft peaks form. Fold melted chocolate, cream and almonds into egg mixture using a slotted spoon. Cut a piece of baking paper to fit the base of the slow cooker bowl. Pour the chocolate mixture into the slow cooker. Cover and cook on LOW for 3–4 hours, or until set.

Dust with icing sugar and serve warm or cold with seasonal fruit such as poached pears, fresh berries, or a raspberry coulis.

Serves 8

sri pinang coconut sago

One of our favourite cheap and cheerful restaurants is called Sri Pinang and if I can ever manage a dessert there, their coconut sago is always my first choice. This is my slow-cooked take on this Malaysian favourite. Palm sugar is available from specialty Asian stores and some supermarkets with an Asian food section. Palm sugar with coconut juice is a different colour from straight palm sugar.

1/2 cup sago
2 1/4 cups boiling water
1/2 cup sugar
400g can coconut cream
palm sugar with coconut juice

Place sago in the slow cooker with boiling water and sugar. Stir to combine. Cover and cook on LOW for 2 hours, stirring halfway through cooking if possible.

Mix in two-thirds of the can of coconut cream. Spoon into individual serving dishes or one large bowl. Grate palm sugar over top. Cool, then refrigerate. When ready to serve, pour remaining coconut milk over and garnish with lime wedges if you wish.

Serves 6

tropical fruit steamed pudding

I made this pudding successfully by spooning the pudding mixture into the cut and tied end of an oven bag then securing the other end and cooking it directly in the slow cooker for 1 1/2 – 2 hours.

125g butter
1/4 cup sugar
2 eggs
1 cup flour
1 teaspoon baking powder
1/2 cup desiccated coconut
1/2 cup passionfruit syrup
1 teaspoon coconut essence
425g can mangoes
passionfruit syrup
cream or yoghurt

Melt butter in a saucepan large enough to mix all ingredients. Remove from heat and add sugar. Mix in eggs until well combined. Sift flour and baking powder into the saucepan and add coconut, passionfruit syrup and coconut essence. Mix with a slotted spoon until combined. Drain mangoes and chop. Fold into the pudding mixture.

Spoon into a greased and baking paper-lined slow cooker bowl. Cover and cook on HIGH for 2 hours or until an inserted skewer comes out clean. Turn onto a plate and serve warm, cut into wedges, with passionfruit syrup and cream or yoghurt.

Serves 4—6

blackberry and apple betty

A 'betty' is one of those old-fashioned delicious puddings everyone seems to have forgotten about. In days gone by when people were much more aware of waste, home-grown fruit and stale bread were used to make this dessert. It is delicious with just about any fruit.

500g frozen blackberries
3 apples
2 cups soft breadcrumbs
1/2 cup dark brown sugar
2 teaspoons grated lemon rind
25g butter
1/2 cup toasted slivered almonds
whipped cream

Thaw berries, reserving juice. Peel apples, core and slice finely. Mix berries and apple slices together. Mix breadcrumbs, brown sugar and lemon rind together. Melt butter and mix into breadcrumb mixture to combine. Grease the slow cooker bowl. Place one-third of the crumb mixture over the base. Spread half the apple mixture over. Continue layering, finishing with a layer of crumbs. Cover and cook on LOW for 6 hours.
  Sprinkle with almonds and serve with whipped cream.

Serves 6

decadent bread and butter pudding

This is one dish that should not be cooked on HIGH as 'eggy' mixtures will curdle.

1 loaf toast bread
butter
1/2 cup orange-flavoured liqueur
or orange juice
1 cup raisins
1/2 cup mixed peel
1 cup apricot jam
6 eggs
3/4 cup sugar
1 cup milk
2 cups cream
1/4 cup dark brown sugar

Cut crusts from bread. Butter each slice thickly on one side. Line the base and sides of the slow cooker with bread, buttered side to the outside. Drizzle orange liqueur or juice over bread. Sprinkle with raisins and mixed peel. Place small dollops of jam over the fruit.

Beat eggs and sugar together until light. Add milk and cream and beat lightly to combine. Pour egg mixture through a fine sieve into the slow cooker. Use remaining bread to cover the top of the pudding, butter side up. Sprinkle dark brown sugar over the top. Cover and cook on LOW for 4–5 hours, or until set. The pudding is cooked when a skewer inserted into the centre comes out clean.

Serve hot with extra whipped cream if you wish.

Serves 6

tip

This pudding cooked perfectly in the slow cooker but it is one recipe that you will need to watch, as it will be more sensitive to high-wattage appliances and fluctuations in voltage during times of heavy power use. Check it an hour before the end of cooking the first time you make it to get a fix on your slow cooker.

very clever impossible pie

Everyone enjoys this pie. It forms a pastry-like crust on the bottom and a custard filling on top as it cooks. It is very clever, and even cleverer in the slow cooker.

1 cup frozen raspberries
4 eggs
1/2 cup flour
1 1/2 cups milk
1 cup sugar
1 cup coconut
2 teaspoons vanilla
cream or yoghurt

Thaw raspberries in a sieve. Combine eggs, flour, milk, sugar, coconut and vanilla in a blender or processor. Mix in raspberries. Cut a piece of baking paper to fit the base of the slow cooker. Pour mixture into the bowl of the slow cooker. Cover and cook on LOW for 2 1/2 – 3 hours or until set.

   Serve warm or cold with cream or yoghurt.

slow-cooked orange-macerated dates and bananas

If you like a little spice in your dessert, mix 1 teaspoon of ground cardamom into the orange juice before pouring over the fruit.

2 cups dates
3 bananas
$^1/_4$ cup dark brown sugar
$^3/_4$ cup orange juice
whipped cream

Break up dates and place half in the bottom of the slow cooker. Peel bananas and cut into 1cm slices. Place a layer of banana slices over dates and sprinkle with half the brown sugar. Repeat the layering. Pour the orange juice over. Cover and cook on LOW for 3–4 hours.
    Serve hot or cold with softly whipped cream.

Serves 4

index